THE STORY OF THE CHICAGO BULLS

Chet Walker

Nikola Vučević

A HISTORY OF HOOPS

THE STORY OF THE

CHICAGO
BULLS

JIM WHITING

CREATIVE SPORTS

Bob Love

CREATIVE EDUCATION / CREATIVE PAPERBACKS

Published by Creative Education and Creative Paperbacks
P.O. Box 227, Mankato, Minnesota 56002
Creative Education and Creative Paperbacks are imprints of
The Creative Company
www.thecreativecompany.us

Design and production by Blue Design (www.bluedes.com)
Art direction by Rita Marshall
Production layout by Rachel Klimpel and Ciara Beitlich

Photographs by AP Images (Tim Boyle, Al Messerschmidt Archive, Jeff
Robbins), Biblio.com (World of Books Ltd.), Getty (Andrew D. Bernstein, Mark
Blinch, Nathaniel S. Butler, Rob Carr, Chicago Tribune, Chris Coduto, Doug
Collier, Lachlan Cunningham, Jonathan Daniel, Focus On Sport, Jeff Haynes,
John Iacono, Icon and Image, Vincent Laforet, Jim McIsaac, Fernando
Medina, Paul Natkin, Herb Scharfman, Carl Skalak), Newscom (Ting Shen),
Shutterstock (Brocreative), Wikimedia Commons (United Press International)

Copyright © 2023 Creative Education, Creative Paperbacks
International copyright reserved in all countries. No part of this book may be
reproduced in any form without written permission from the publisher.

Library of Congress Cataloging-in-Publication Data
Names: Whiting, Jim, 1943- author.
Title: The story of the Chicago Bulls / by Jim Whiting.
Description: Mankato, Minnesota : Creative Education/ Creative Paperbacks,
   [2023] | Series: Creative Sports: A History of Hoops | Includes index. |
   Audience: Ages 8-12 | Audience: Grades 4-6 | Summary: "Middle grade
   basketball fans are introduced to the extraordinary history of NBA's
   Chicago Bulls with a photo-laden narrative of their greatest successes and
   losses"-- Provided by publisher.
Identifiers: LCCN 2022007529 (print) | LCCN 2022007530 (ebook) | ISBN
   9781640266216 (library binding) | ISBN 9781682771778 (paperback) | ISBN
   9781640007628 (ebook)
Subjects: LCSH: Chicago Bulls (Basketball team)--History--Juvenile literature.
Classification: LCC GV885.52.C45 W553 2023 (print) | LCC GV885.52.C45 (ebook)
   | DDC 796.323/640977311--dc23/eng/20220518
LC record available at https://lccn.loc.gov/2022007529
LC ebook record available at https://lccn.loc.gov/2022007530

Horace Grant

CONTENTS

LEGENDS OF THE HARDWOOD

Michael Jordan's last shot of his Bulls career

GOING OUT ON TOP

The Chicago Bulls stood on the verge of history as the 1997–98 National Basketball Association (NBA) regular season ended. No team had won three straight championships twice since the Boston Celtics took eight straight titles between 1958 and 1966. To accomplish their second three-peat, the Bulls had to defeat the Utah Jazz in the NBA Finals. The Bulls had a 3-games-to-2 lead. In the final moments of Game 6, the Jazz led by three points. If they won, the final game would be played on their home court before their rabid fans. Bulls shooting guard Michael Jordan scored on a lay-in with 37 seconds left. That narrowed Utah's margin to a single point. With the shot clock winding down, burly Utah power forward Karl Malone took a pass in the low post. Jordan stripped the ball and dribbled downcourt. "We all knew what was coming next," said basketball writer Mitch Lawrence. "It was just a matter of how Jordan would do it." Utah small forward Bryon Russell, perhaps his team's best defender, picked up Jordan at the top of the key. Jordan's teammates cleared out space for him. He dribbled to his right, then suddenly accelerated. Russell slipped and fell backward onto the court. He desperately tried to scramble to his feet. Too late. Jordan pulled up and launched a 15-foot jump shot with 5.2 seconds remaining. No doubt about it. Jordan raised his right arm in triumph. It was his last basket as a Bulls player. He announced his retirement soon afterward. Many people consider him the greatest basketball player in history. Certainly, he is the most famous.

Jerry Sloan

LEGENDS
OF THE HARDWOOD

JOHNNY KERR
COACH
BULLS SEASONS:
1966–68

JERRY SLOAN
SHOOTING GUARD/
SMALL FORWARD
HEIGHT: 6-FOOT-5
BULLS SEASONS:
1966–76

LOCAL GUYS MAKE GOOD

Johnny Kerr started playing basketball his
senior year in high school. He led his team to
the 1950 Chicago Public League championship.
Later, he helped the Syracuse Nationals
capture the 1955 NBA championship. He became
Chicago's first coach. Then he served as a Bulls
broadcaster for 33 years. Jerry Sloan grew up
on a farm in southern Illinois. He got up at 4:30
a.m. to do chores. Then he walked two miles
to school for 7:00 a.m. practice. He helped
the University of Evansville win two straight
Division II titles. Sloan was called the "original
Bull" after spending 10 years with the team.
He was the first Bull to have his jersey number
retired. Both men will always have honored
places in Bulls' lore.

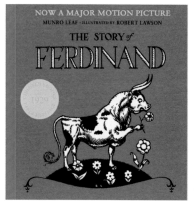

The Bulls weren't the first professional basketball team in the "Windy City." The Chicago Stags played four years between 1946 and 1950. The Chicago Packers began playing in 1961. They lost 62 games. Fans stayed away. Changing their name to the Zephyrs the following season didn't help. They lost 55 games. Chicago businessman Dick Klein wanted to buy the team and keep it in Chicago. He couldn't. The Zephyrs moved to Baltimore. Klein didn't give up. He asked the NBA to let him start an expansion team. The league agreed. He paid $1.6 million in 1966 for his franchise. His family thought up the nickname in their living room. Klein's son Greg recalled, "We'd be playing in the International Amphitheater near the stockyards," he said. "We were throwing around one-syllable names to fit in with the Cubs, Sox, Bears . . . But the best I can recall us coming up with was 'Steers.' Then my younger brother, Mark, came into the room with one of his favorite children's books, *The Story of Ferdinand*." A bull is the central character in that book. So, Bulls it was. They are strong animals with a never-say-die attitude.

The Bulls lived up to their name right away. Chicago played the St. Louis Hawks in their first game. Hawks player/coach Richie Guerin said the Bulls would be lucky to win 10 games. The Bulls made him eat his words. They won that night and three of their next four games. "I thought, 'My goodness, we're not that good, are we?'" said forward/guard Jerry Sloan before the next game. "We certainly found out that night. The Knicks waxed us pretty good, and reality started to set in."

Chicago had an eight-game losing streak in November. They sank to last place by the end of February. On March 1, the Bulls hosted the Philadelphia 76ers. The Sixers would go on to win 68 regular-season games and the NBA championship. Somehow, the Bulls posted a 129–122 victory that night. That spurred Chicago to win 7 of its final 11 games. The Bulls finished 33–48. Despite the losing record, they qualified for the playoffs. No expansion team had ever made the playoffs in its first year. It hasn't happened since then either. Bulls coach Johnny Kerr was voted Coach of the Year. But St. Louis swept the Bulls in the first round.

The Bulls had losing records for the next three years. In 1970–71, coach Dick Motta led Chicago to a 51–31 mark. The team surpassed the 50-win mark the next three years as well. Led by Sloan and scrappy point/shooting guard Norm Van Lier, Chicago developed a reputation for tough defense. "Playing the Bulls is like running through a barbed wire fence," said Los Angeles Lakers guard Gail Goodrich. "You may win the game, but they're gonna put lumps on you."

The Bulls advanced to the conference finals in 1974 and 1975. Both times they could go no further. Chicago dropped to 24 wins in 1975–76. Motta was fired. After a brief revival led by 7-foot-2 center Artis Gilmore, the Bulls plunged to 31 wins in 1978–79. They were just as bad the following year. The Bulls rebounded to win 45 games and reach the second round of the playoffs in 1980–81. Yet they fell back to 34–48 the following season. They traded Gilmore. The result was obvious. "Lack of a dominating center is the major reason [the Bulls] have lost 111 games in the last 2 seasons," wrote the *Chicago Tribune* before the 1984 NBA Draft.

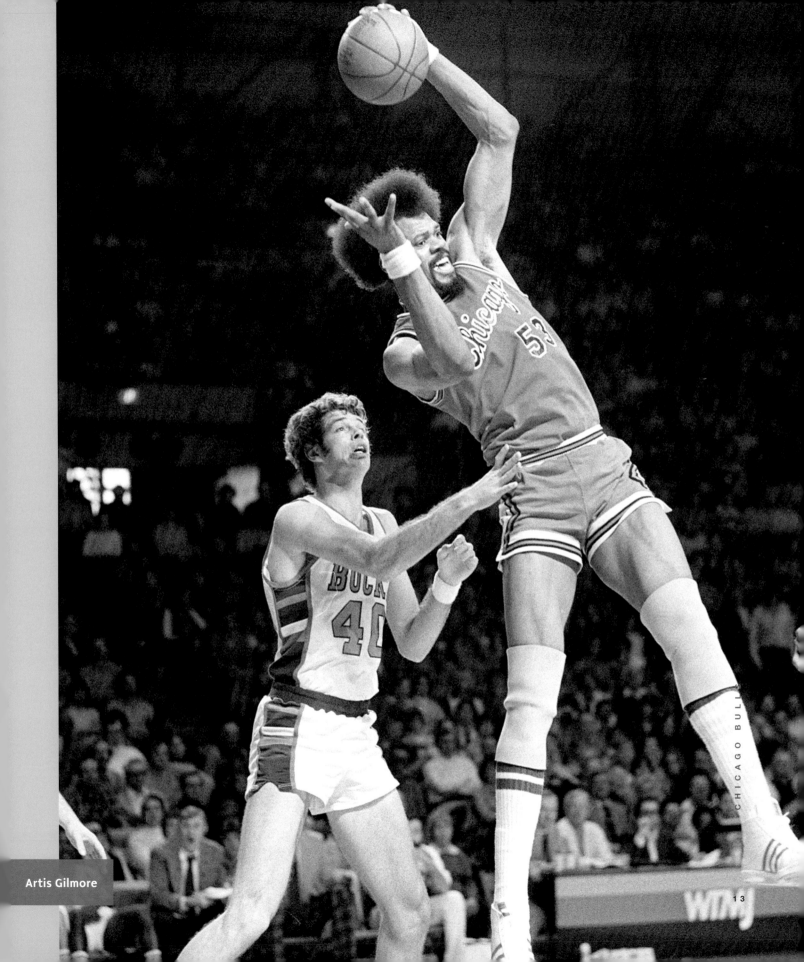

Artis Gilmore

MICHAEL JORDAN ARRIVES

Chicago wanted a big man to replace Gilmore. Houston had the first pick. They took center Hakeem "The Dream" Olajuwon. Portland drafted second. They chose 7-foot-1 shot blocker and rebounder Sam Bowie. Rod Thorn, Chicago's general manager, was disappointed. Chicago had the third pick. Thorn tried to trade that pick for an established center. He couldn't. Somewhat reluctantly, he chose Michael Jordan. "We wish he were seven feet tall, but he isn't," Thorn said at the time. "There just wasn't a center available. What can you do?" It didn't take long for Jordan to show what he could do. He was NBA Rookie of the Year after averaging 28.2 points per game. Most players would be delighted with such a high average. It is a measure of Jordan's greatness that it is the *lowest* average of the 11 times he played a full season. He soon earned the nicknames "Air Jordan" and "His Airness." He could remain airborne longer than anyone else.

Despite losing records the next two years, the Bulls made the playoffs. Both times they were swept in three games. Jordan scored 63 points against the Boston Celtics in 1986. It was a playoff record. The following season, he became the second player in NBA history to score 3,000 points in a season. He also proved to be more than just a scoring machine. He was an outstanding defender as well. That same season he became the first NBA player with 200 steals and 100 blocked shots.

Michael Jordan

THREE-PEAT I

The Bulls crafted one of their most successful drafts in 1987. They chose power forward/center Horace Grant. He would have seven productive seasons in Chicago. They also traded Olden Polynice to the Seattle SuperSonics and got small forward Scottie Pippen in return. "I never heard of him or his school [the University of Central Arkansas]," Jordan said. Soon the entire country heard of Pippen. He became a key contributor as Chicago won 50 games. Jordan was named Most Valuable Player (MVP), Defensive Player of the Year, and All-Star Game MVP. The Bulls, though, lost to the Detroit Pistons in the playoffs. The Pistons were known as the "Bad Boys" for their aggressive playing style.

The Bulls had one of the most memorable plays in their history in the 1988–89 playoffs. They trailed the Cleveland Cavaliers by one point in the final moments of the deciding game in the first round. Jordan took a contested inbound pass and dribbled toward the foul line. With one second left, he leaped for a jump shot. He seemed to suspend himself in midair as his defender flew past him. Then he let go of the ball. Nothing but net! Chicago won 101–100. Jordan's jump for joy after sinking the shot became famous. Since then, his game-winner has been known simply as "The Shot." But the Bulls lost to the Pistons again in the conference finals.

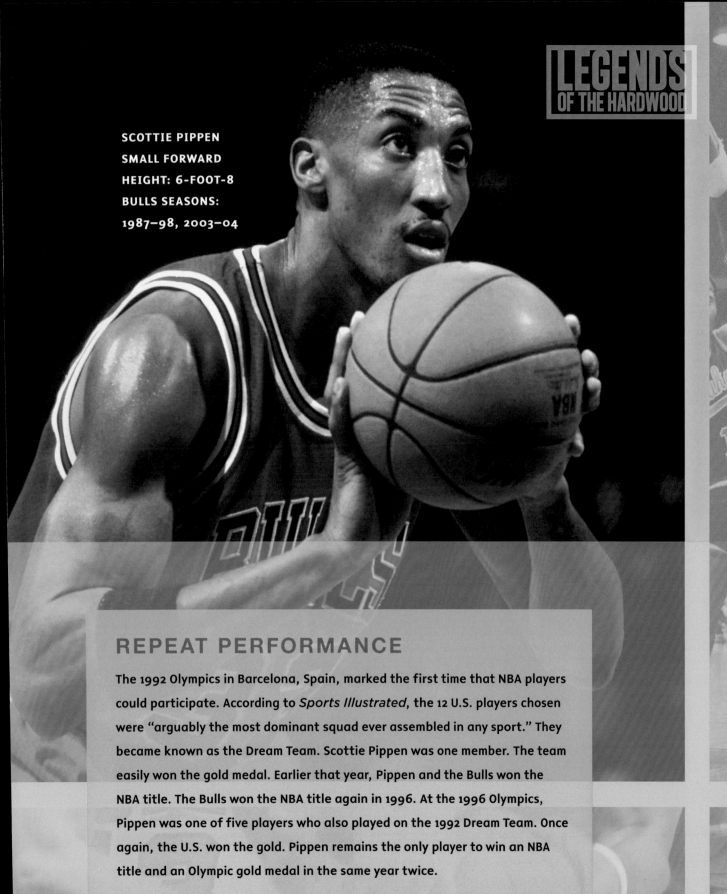

SCOTTIE PIPPEN
SMALL FORWARD
HEIGHT: 6-FOOT-8
BULLS SEASONS:
1987–98, 2003–04

CHICAGO BULLS

REPEAT PERFORMANCE

The 1992 Olympics in Barcelona, Spain, marked the first time that NBA players could participate. According to *Sports Illustrated*, the 12 U.S. players chosen were "arguably the most dominant squad ever assembled in any sport." They became known as the Dream Team. Scottie Pippen was one member. The team easily won the gold medal. Earlier that year, Pippen and the Bulls won the NBA title. The Bulls won the NBA title again in 1996. At the 1996 Olympics, Pippen was one of five players who also played on the 1992 Dream Team. Once again, the U.S. won the gold. Pippen remains the only player to win an NBA title and an Olympic gold medal in the same year twice.

Michael Jordan and Scottie Pippen

Phil Jackson stepped in as coach in 1989. He guided the team to a 55–27 mark. Once again, Chicago couldn't get past the Pistons in the playoffs.

Three years of frustration ended the following year. After winning an NBA-best 61 games, the Bulls swept Detroit in the conference finals. "They got in our head with the physical stuff," Pippen said of the three earlier playoff defeats. "But in doing it, the Pistons taught us the toughness we needed." Jordan and Pippen steered the Bulls past the Los Angeles Lakers to claim their first NBA title. The Bulls were even better the following season. Their 67 wins were the best in team history. They stomped over Portland in the Finals. In 1992–93, Jordan won his seventh scoring title in a row. Many people thought the Phoenix Suns would win the NBA title. The Bulls didn't. They defeated the Suns in six games. Winning three titles in a row became known as a "three-peat."

Many fans thought that Chicago could win four titles in a row. They were stunned when Jordan announced his retirement before the start of the 1993–94 season. He was just 30 years old and obviously at the peak of his game. He wanted to play professional baseball. Chicago still won 55 games without him. But the Bulls lost to the New York Knicks in the playoffs.

Dennis Rodman

CHICAGO BULLS

PHIL JACKSON
HEAD COACH
BULLS SEASONS:
1989–98

WORKING THE ANGLES

Phil Jackson played 12 years as a power forward between 1967 and 1980, mostly with the Knicks. In 1987, the Bulls hired him as an assistant coach. He became head coach two years later, in 1989–90. Michael Jordan was beginning to emerge as a superstar. Jackson introduced the "triangle offense." It involved spacing the players—especially Jordan—on the court to take advantage of their strong points. Chicago made it to the Eastern Conference finals in Jackson's first season. They lost in seven games to their archrival Detroit Pistons. They won the title in 1990–91 and the following two seasons. This is called a "three-peat." The Bulls had another "three-peat" from 1996–98. Jackson left the team after his sixth title. Chicago had six losing seasons in a row without him. They haven't come close to winning another title since. Jackson went on to coach the Los Angeles Lakers and won five more titles. His 11 NBA championships as a coach are the most of all time.

THREE-PEAT II

Jordan returned late in the 1994–95 season. He helped the Bulls advance to the Eastern Conference semifinals. But the Bulls bowed out to the Orlando Magic in six games. Some people said that Jordan wasn't as good as he had been. He wanted to prove them wrong. He trained especially hard for the following season. He received help from an unexpected direction. Former Detroit "Bad Boy" Dennis Rodman joined the team at power forward. His fierce defense and rebounding helped the Bulls win an all-time NBA-best 72 games. The Bulls beat the Seattle SuperSonics in six games to win their fourth NBA title.

Chicago won 69 games the following season and repeated as NBA champions. They knocked off the Jazz the following season to secure their second three-peat.

Jordan wasn't the only missing face when the Bulls opened the 1998–99 season. Coach Jackson also left. The team traded Pippen and released Rodman. In addition, the team's draft picks during the 1990s hadn't turned out well. The Bulls had no replacements for their stars. Chicago plummeted to 13–37 in the lockout-shortened 1998–99 season. Toni Kukoc was one bright spot. He led the team in scoring, rebounds, and assists. Chicago traded him when the season ended. Power forward/center Elton Brand shared NBA Rookie of the Year honors in 1999–2000, but the team finished 17–65. Chicago was even worse the following year. They played seven rookies and stumbled to a franchise-worst 15–67. The next three years weren't much better. Sometimes non-basketball issues arose. The Bulls drafted point guard Jay Williams with the second overall pick in the 2002 NBA Draft. After a good rookie season, Williams crashed his motorcycle. His injuries ended his NBA career.

THE BULLS STAMPEDE AGAIN

Under coach Scott Skiles, the Bulls turned things around in 2004–05. Their 47 victories more than doubled the total from the previous year. One key was the play of second-year point guard Kirk Hinrich. He and shifty shooting guard Ben Gordon gave Chicago one of the league's best backcourts. The improved play of small forward Luol Deng helped propel Chicago to the 2006–07 Eastern Conference semifinals. The Bulls lost to Detroit, 4 games to 2. The team got off to a bad start the following year. Skiles was fired. The Bulls stumbled to a 33–49 record.

That dismal mark had one consolation. Chicago gained the top pick in the 2008 NBA Draft. The Bulls chose point guard Derrick Rose. He was voted NBA Rookie of the Year. After two straight 41–41 seasons, Chicago hired defensive specialist Tom Thibodeau as coach. Thibodeau guided the Bulls to the top spot in the Eastern Conference in 2010–11. Chicago won 62 games. That tied the record for a rookie coach. Rose was named MVP. At 22 years, 191 days, he was the youngest player to win the award. But LeBron James and the Miami Heat burned Chicago in five games in the conference finals.

LEGENDS OF THE HARDWOOD

CHICAGO VS. INDIANA
EASTERN CONFERENCE FINALS
GAME 7
MAY 31, 1998

CLOSE CALL

The Bulls nearly didn't get the chance to play for their second three-peat in 1997–98. They had to get by the Indiana Pacers in the Eastern Conference finals. The series went the full seven games. Game 7 was hard-fought and had several lead changes. Midway through the fourth quarter, Indiana surged in front 77–74. Then some Indiana defensive confusion gave point guard Steve Kerr a wide-open look. He sank a three-point shot to tie the score. "That was the turning point," said Indiana shooting guard Fred Hoiberg. "The roof flew off the place." Chicago inched ahead. They played great defense and snagged some key rebounds. They won 88–83. "That was the scariest game we ever faced," Kerr said.

CHICAGO BULLS

LEGENDS
OF THE HARDWOOD

DERRICK ROSE

POINT GUARD

HEIGHT: 6-FOOT-2

BULLS SEASONS: 2008–16

A ROSE THAT NEVER FULLY BLOOMED

It's hard to find any player with a more spectacular start than Derrick Rose. In the first round of the 2011–12 playoffs, Chicago held a 12-point lead over Philadelphia with just over a minute remaining. They were obviously going to win. Yet Rose was still in the game. He went up for a jump shot and came down awkwardly. He had suffered a severe knee injury. He missed the entire 2012–13 season. "His career has never been the same," said sportswriter Matthew Schmidt. "Gone is Rose's signature explosiveness and unreal athleticism." Many basketball authorities rank Rose as the Bulls' best all-time point guard. They can only speculate what he might have done if he hadn't suffered the injury.

An owners' lockout shortened the following season. Chicago still won 50 games. The Bulls had high hopes for the playoffs, but Rose suffered a serious knee injury in the first round. Chicago lost to the 76ers. Rose missed the entire 2012–13 season. The Bulls still won 45 games and advanced to the second round of the playoffs.

With Rose playing just 10 games, the Bulls made the playoffs again in 2013–14. But they lost in the first round. Things looked better in 2014–15. Small forward Jimmy Butler was named the NBA's Most Improved Player. Center Joakim Noah, 2014 Defensive Player of the Year, anchored the middle. Chicago won 50 games. But they lost to the Cleveland Cavaliers in the Eastern Conference semifinals.

Jimmy Butler

Rose began the 2015–16 season with yet another injury—a fractured cheekbone. The Bulls finished with 42 wins. They missed the playoffs. Rose was traded. The team managed a 41–41 record in 2016–17 and made the playoffs. Chicago fans were thrilled when the Bulls won the first two games against the top-seeded Celtics. They couldn't maintain the momentum. Boston easily won the next four. Butler left. After that, the Bulls struggled for several seasons. They improved in 2020–21 under new coach Billy Donovan.

ZACH LAVINE
SHOOTING GUARD/
SMALL FORWARD
HEIGHT: 6-FOOT-5
BULLS SEASONS: 2017–PRESENT

A TALENT OUT OF THIS WORLD

When Zach LaVine was five years old, he watched the movie *Space Jam* on videotape. In the film, Michael Jordan leads some cartoon characters in a game against a team of hulking Monstars from outer space. LaVine became obsessed. "It would finish, and he would just turn it back on," said his father. Within a year he had worn out the tape. LaVine brought the same enthusiasm to real basketball as he grew older. He put in countless hours in his backyard, perfecting his moves. He usually finished with a series of dunks. The hard work paid off. He was named Washington State's best prep player in 2013. He attended UCLA for a year. Minnesota drafted him in 2014. He won the NBA's slam dunk contest in his first two seasons. He was traded to Chicago before the 2017–18 season. In Minnesota, LaVine had averaged more than 13 points a game. As a Bull, he averaged more than 24 points a game. He was named to two All-Star Games.

CHICAGO BULLS

Things got better in 2021–22. Chicago added point guard Lonzo Ball. He quickly made his mark, notching a triple-double in the season's third game. The Bulls also added four-time All-Star DeMar DeRozan. He and swingman Zach LaVine traded team high-point honors for much of the season. Veteran center Nikola Vučević averaged 17.6 points and 11 rebounds per game in his first full season in Chicago. The Bulls finished 46–36. It was their first winning record in six seasons. They faced the Bucks in the first round of the playoffs. The teams split the first two games, but Milwaukee won the next three to end Chicago's season.

During their more than five decades of existence, the Chicago Bulls have had their ups and downs. Those ups have included some of the NBA's greatest moments. The Bulls boast six championship banners. Only the Lakers, Celtics, and Warriors have more. Fans hope that the new generation of Bulls can rise to the same heights. Nothing would make them happier than a third three-peat.

DeMar DeRozan

INDEX

Lonzo Ball